Islands
INSIDE OUT

Megan Kopp

CRABTREE
Publishing Company
www.crabtreebooks.com

Author: Megan Kopp
Publishing plan research
and series development: Reagan Miller
Editors: Sarah Eason, Jennifer Sanderson
and Shirley Duke
Proofreaders: Katie Dicker, Wendy Scavuzzo
Editorial director: Kathy Middleton
Design: Paul Myerscough
Cover design: Paul Myerscough
Photo research: Jennifer Sanderson
Production coordinator and
Prepress technician: Tammy McGarr
Print coordinator: Katherine Berti

Written and designed for Crabtree Publishing
by Calcium Creative

Library and Archives Canada Cataloguing in Publication

Kopp, Megan, author
        Islands inside out / Megan Kopp.

(Ecosystems inside out)
Includes index.
Issued in print and electronic formats.
ISBN 978-0-7787-1497-2 (bound).--
ISBN 978-0-7787-1501-6 (pbk.).--
ISBN 978-1-4271-7657-8 (pdf).--ISBN 978-1-4271-7653-0 (html)

        1. Island ecology--Juvenile literature. 2. Island animals--
Juvenile literature. I. Title.

QH541.5.I8K67 2015   j577.5'2   C2014-907853-6
                                                C2014-907854-4

Library of Congress Cataloging-in-Publication Data

CIP available at the Library of Congress

Crabtree Publishing Company

www.crabtreebooks.com   1-800-387-7650

Printed in Canada/022015/IH20141209

Published in Canada
Crabtree Publishing
616 Welland Ave.
St. Catharines, Ontario
L2M 5V6

Published in the United States
Crabtree Publishing
PMB 59051
350 Fifth Avenue, 59th Floor
New York, New York 10118

Published in the United Kingdom
Crabtree Publishing
Maritime House
Basin Road North, Hove
BN41 1WR

Published in Australia
Crabtree Publishing
3 Charles Street
Coburg North
VIC, 3058

Contents

What Is an Ecosystem?

Survival on Earth depends on both living and nonliving things. Sunshine, water, air, soil, and temperature are nonliving things necessary for survival. They are called **abiotic factors**. Living things are called **biotic factors**. Biotic factors include plants and animals. An ecosystem is made up of **organisms**, the environment in which they live, and their **interrelationships**.

Ecosystems Vary Greatly in Size

An ecosystem can be as small as a puddle, or as large as an ocean. A **biome** is a large geographical area that contains similar plants, animals, and environments. Oceans, wetlands, and rain forests are examples of a few of Earth's biomes.

What Is an Island?

Islands are areas of land surrounded entirely by water. However, Australia is an exception to the rule. Due to its vast size, most people consider Australia to be a **continent** like North America, rather than an island. Islands can be found in oceans, seas, lakes, and rivers. Islands are created by volcanic eruptions, waves and sand, **coral reefs**, or the shifting of continents. Many of the plant and animal **species** found on islands are unique because of their **isolation**, or separation, from other landmasses.

Let's explore the ecosystems found on the islands of the world. We will look at each ecosystem as a whole and explore one part of it further.

What Is a System?

A system is a group of separate parts that work together for a purpose. Ecosystems are made up of plants, animals, water, soil, air, and other biotic and abiotic factors. Each part has an important role to play in the overall health of the ecosystem. Many of these individual parts are interdependent. It is a fine balance. If just one part of the ecosystem changes, the whole system can be affected.

This map shows where islands and other biomes are found around the world.

Key

- Mountains—ranges
- ▲ Mountains—land peaks
- ▲ Mountains—sea peaks
- Forests—temperate
- Forests—taiga
- Forests—tropical
- ∿ Rivers and Lakes
- Islands

Only 3 percent of Earth's land surfaces are islands, but islands are home to 20 percent of all of Earth's known bird, **reptile**, and plant species.

Energy in Ecosystems

sun

Energy in an ecosystem starts with the sun. It spreads throughout the ecosystem as food. Plants use the energy of the sun to grow. Other animals eat the plants to gain energy. Organisms eat other types of organisms to survive. This is called a **food chain**. Many different organisms rely on a single food chain.

Energy Flow

Living things in an ecosystem are producers, consumers, or decomposers. Plants are producers. They use energy from the sun to make their own food through a process called **photosynthesis**. Animals are consumers. They must eat food to get the energy they need to survive. Animals that eat plants are called herbivores. Carnivores are meat-eaters. These animals eat other animals for food. Omnivores eat both plants and animals.

Decomposers, such as **fungi** and **bacteria**, break down plant and animal material. They are nature's cleanup crew. They put the **nutrients** back into the soil so that plants keep growing and the food chain continues.

Food Webs

Everything is connected in an ecosystem. The energy from one food chain flows to living things in many other food chains. When two or more food chains connect, they become a **food web**. Healthy food webs need plenty of sunshine, good soil, and a lot of water. A healthy food web has many producers and fewer consumers.

plants → **iguana** → **snake** → **hawk**

This food chain shows the flow of energy from one organism to another.

Galápagos penguins enjoy a variety of foods that they find in the waters around them. They eat small fish such as mullet and sardines.

Eco Up Close

Water is an important abiotic factor in island ecosystems. It changes form and moves around the world through a process called the water cycle. The water cycle includes **evaporation**, **condensation**, and **precipitation**.

Water can transform an island ecosystem. Hawaii's Big Island has a dry side and a wet side. Water evaporates from the ocean. Winds push clouds over the high, middle section of the island. Water condenses and drops as precipitation on the wet side. Very different species can be found on each side of the island.

Galápagos Islands

The Galápagos Islands are found approximately 600 miles (965 km) west of the Ecuadorian **mainland**. The islands are home to many species not found anywhere else in the world. These unique species are **endemic** to the islands. The islands have 830 miles (1,336 km) of coastline.

Giants on the Loose

On land, there is little competition for food, and few **predators**. Predators are animals that hunt other animals for food. Galápagos tortoises grow abnormally large. This is known as island **gigantism**. They weigh nearly 600 pounds (272 kg) and live longer than most humans. The islands are also home to the world's largest cormorant. It is also the only cormorant unable to fly. Scalesias are plants related to sunflowers. There are few insects or **rodents** to eat the flowers, so the scalesias have grown larger over time. They are now 20 to 30 feet (6 to 9 m) tall.

Alien Invasion

Since the islands were discovered in 1535, humans have brought new species to them, accidentally and on purpose. Goats and donkeys are **invasive species** brought to the Galápagos by humans. They **reproduce** quickly and eat plants that **native** species need to live. One-quarter of Galápagos plant species and half of the animal species are **endangered** as a result of early human activity on the islands. Endangered means to be at risk of dying out.

Three major ocean **currents** meet at the islands, bringing an incredible mix of life.

Eco Focus

In 1978, the Galápagos were declared the first World Heritage Site because of the rich wildlife there. More than 100,000 tourists visit the islands each year and this is putting a strain on this unique environment. How do you think this increase in tourism affects plants and animals on the Galápagos? What can be done to help reduce this impact? Explain your answers.

Eco Up Close

Galápagos finches are one of the most interesting groups of birds on the Galápagos. The scientist Charles Darwin was fascinated by these birds. There was no competition or threat from other small birds, so the finches **adapted** to eat different foods. Those finches that eat hard-shelled fruits and nuts have large beaks. Those that feed on cactus flowers have thin beaks. There are now at least 13 species of finches on the Galápagos. They all **evolved**, or changed slowly over time, from the same original species.

Galápagos finch

Florida Keys

A key is a small, sandy island with low **elevation** on a coral reef. Keys, also known as cayes or cays, are found throughout the Pacific, Atlantic, and Indian Oceans. The Florida Keys are a long chain of around 1,700 islands running south from mainland Florida to the Dry Tortugas, which are 68 miles (109 km) west of Key West.

Florida's low elevation Keys are often flooded by saltwater during **tropical** storms and hurricanes.

How the Keys Formed

The upper Keys were formed by a coral reef that was exposed 100,000 years ago. The lower Keys are made of a harder limestone rock created by evaporation of the saltwater. Most areas of the Keys are only 4 to 6 feet (1.2 to 1.8 m) above sea level. The shorelines are fringed with mangroves and other **salt-tolerant plants**. Salt-tolerant plants are those that can grow in salty water.

A Home for Birds and Deer

Brown pelicans and other seabirds nest in the mangroves. Higher elevations are covered with hardwood trees and other plant species. This **habitat** is used by the endangered Key deer for feeding. Key deer feast on more than 150 different species of plants. In the heat of the day, the deer find shelter in mangrove swamps. Habitat loss, getting hit by cars on roadways, and **climate change** and its effects on mangroves are the biggest threats, or dangers, facing Key deer.

brown pelican

Eco Up Close

Brown pelicans are large seabirds with an average wingspan of more than 6.5 feet (2 m). They can be found along the coast in southern North America and northern South America. They live along the ocean coast, preferring shallow waters, such as those found along the Keys. Diving headlong into the water from a height of 20 to 30 feet (6 to 9 m), the birds hunt for fish. They scoop up their **prey** and gallons of water in a pouch. When the birds go back to the surface, they lower their bill to drain out the water, and then gulp down any fish caught in the pouch. Brown pelicans were once endangered in the United States as a result of **pesticide** poisoning. Since the pesticide DDT was banned, the species has recovered on the east coast of the United States.

Barrier Islands

Barrier islands are long, narrow strips of sand that are separated from the mainland by **estuaries**, bays, or **lagoons**. They are called barrier islands because they help block winds and ocean waves that might reach the mainland. A wide, sandy beach on the ocean side of the island leads to sand dunes anchored, or held down, by grasses and shrubs. Barrier islands are common along coasts of the United States.

Assateague is a barrier island along the Atlantic coast. Like most barrier islands, it is constantly being reshaped by ocean currents and storms.

How Barrier Islands Form

Barrier islands can form in two ways. Sand sometimes builds up offshore. When these underwater dunes break the water surface, they can become barrier islands. Changes in sea levels also create barrier islands. When sea levels rise, inland dunes can be separated from the mainland. This creates an island.

Life on Barrier Islands

Life along the beaches of barrier islands can be harsh. Most of the animal life can be found in the dunes off the beach. Small patches of plants grow in wind-sheltered areas. This plant life provides shelter and food for island wildlife.

Barrier islands are important for shorebirds such as sandpipers. Sandpipers cruise the surf edge, feeding on crabs and other **invertebrates** (animals without backbones). Raccoons and foxes patrol the **upper tide line** and dunes in search of food. The upper tide line is the line on the shore where high tide normally reaches. Insects, mice, and snakes live in the dunes.

Eco Focus

Barrier islands are unique ecosystems. They provide feeding, mating, and nesting areas for many species. These sea-lined dunes are also popular places to build recreational properties. Should barrier islands be protected from such building? Explain your thinking.

Eco Up Close

Wild horses can be found on Assateague. Mainland owners looking to avoid fencing laws and livestock taxes brought the horses to the island more than 300 years ago. They have survived severe weather and low-quality food. As a result of this poor diet, the horses are now only the size of ponies. **Overgrazing** by the horses can lead to erosion, or wearing away, of the sand dunes. This affects the entire ecosystem.

wild horse

The Caribbean

The Caribbean Islands are mainly coral islands. Coral are tiny sea animals that build hard skeletons of **calcium carbonate** outside their bodies. Over time, these skeletons form mounds or ridges. Eventually, they break the ocean surface. Rock, sand, and other living material help create the island. Some of the larger Caribbean islands include Cuba, Hispaniola, Jamaica, Puerto Rico, and Trinidad.

The Caribbean Islands stretch across more than 1.5 million square miles (4 million sq km) of ocean and include more than 7,000 islands.

Island Wonderworld

The Caribbean Islands have close to 13,000 different species of plants. Cuba has more than 6,500 plant species. Half of these are endemic to Cuba, and are not found anywhere else in the world. Hundreds of species of animals found in the Caribbean are endemic, including nearly half of the 90 species of mammals, more than one quarter of the more than 600 species of birds, and nearly all of the 500 reptile species.

Under Threat

Introduced species such as rats, cats, dogs, goats, donkeys, and monkeys have had a devastating effect on the island ecosystems. These animals prey on native species, eat their food, and destroy their habitat. As a result, nearly all of the **amphibian** species on Haiti are threatened with extinction. Cutting down too many trees is another problem on the islands. The Grenada dove is endemic to the Caribbean island of Grenada. It lives in dry forest, which is being cut down to build hotels for tourists. The species is now critically endangered.

Caribbean fruit bat

Eco Up Close

Caribbean fruit bats are a **subspecies** of Jamaican fruit bats. They are found on several islands including Cuba, Bahamas, Turks and Caicos, Grand Cayman, Cayman Brac, and Little Cayman. These bats eat wild fruits such as Indian almond tree seeds and Christmas palm berries. Bats do not digest the seeds and they are **excreted**. This helps spread the seeds throughout the islands, keeping the forests **diverse** and healthy.

Hawaiian Islands

The Hawaiian Islands were formed by volcanic eruptions in the ocean floor. The islands existed in isolation for almost 70 million years. There are very diverse ecosystems, ranging from tropical dry forests to **subalpine** grasslands and underground lava tubes. This allows for a wide variety of native animal and plant species to evolve, including five unique species of hibiscus, and eyeless animals adapted to life in the dark.

On the Edge

There were no reptiles, amphibians, ants, honeybees, earthworms, parrots, hummingbirds, seagulls, pine trees, or coconut palms on the islands before the arrival of humans. However, because of these introduced species and habitat loss, Hawaii is sometimes called the "extinction capital of the world."

Bird Heaven

Hawaii was paradise for birds. There were no mammals or reptiles on the islands to begin with, so there were no ground predators. If a hawk threatened overhead, songbirds dropped to the ground and found cover for safety. As they had no need to fly, over time, many species lost their ability to fly. However, the introduction of predators to the islands has wiped out the flightless and ground-nesting species.

Eco Focus

Half of Hawaii's animals are extinct. One of the biggest causes of this is the introduction of **alien** species such as rats, dogs, and pigs. About 140 bird species native to the Hawaiian Islands before the arrival of humans have become extinct. What do you think Hawaiian ecosystems would look like today if the alien species had never been introduced? Explain your thinking.

16

Nearly all of the native plants of Hawaii are endemic to the islands.

The Hawaiian green sea turtle is the world's largest hard-shelled sea turtle. Adult turtles can weigh up to 330 pounds (150 kg) and their shells often reach 40 inches (102 cm) in length. These turtles are herbivores, feeding mainly on algae. Green sea turtles are often found basking in the sun on beaches in Hawaii. These turtles are endangered partly because the algae habitats are slowly being degraded.

Hawaiian green sea turtle

Aleutian Archipelago

A string of islands is known as an archipelago. The Aleutian Islands Archipelago runs from the Alaska Peninsula 1,100 miles (1,770 km) southwest then northwest, between the Bering Sea and the Gulf of Alaska. It includes more than 300 islands formed by volcanic eruptions.

A Rugged Home

The rocky landscape of the Aleutian Archipelago is home to millions of birds, but no trees. Plant life includes grasses, flowers, and shrubs such as willow and crowberry. Aleutian plants rely on seabird droppings, called guano, for nutrients. Large colonies, or groups, of seabirds can be found on the islands. The Pribilof Islands provide a breeding habitat for close to 3 million seabirds. Introduced species such as cattle, reindeer, and fox that now live on the islands have become feral, or wild. Grazing and hunting by these species is affecting the seabirds and endemic species, such as the endangered Pribilof Island shrew.

Cold Waters Full of Life

The cold waters around the Aleutian Islands are very busy! More than 450 species of fish are found in the region. These fish feed the seabirds. **Commercial fishing** has reduced fish numbers and harms the ecosystem. Trawlers rake the seabed and destroy the ecosystem, which affects the birds that rely on an abundance of fish. Protecting the ocean is vital for protecting life on these islands.

The Aleutian Islands are a harsh environment with little ground cover for wildlife.

Eco Up Close

The Aleutian Islands provide a breeding habitat for almost all of the world's 250,000 red-legged kittiwakes. More than three quarters of these birds nest on St. George Island. The gulls spend winters at sea, returning in spring to nest on sea cliffs. There are fewer kittiwakes today, but the reasons for this are not fully known. It may be a result of **overfishing** by people, which reduces food availability. Overfishing is taking more fish than the ecosystem can replace. The recent building of a harbor in the Pribilof Islands has increased the risk of rats being accidentally introduced. Rats will eat seabird eggs and unprotected young birds.

red-legged kittiwake

Islands of Japan

Japan's islands are among the most active volcanic islands in the world. The islands sit on four **tectonic plates.** The two heavier plates are slowly slipping under the two lighter plates, causing volcanic and earthquake activity. The islands of Japan are close to 145,000 square miles (375,550 sq km) in total. The country's 6,000 or so islands stretch for more than 1,864 miles (3,000 km) from north to south. As a result, there are many different ecosystems.

Animals and Plants of Japan

Japan has 160 species of mammals including the goat-like antelope called the serow, giant flying squirrel, Japanese bear, and wild boar. There are 700 species of birds on the islands including bush warblers, swallows, and pheasants, which are commonly found there. The islands are also home to 32,000 species of insects—many of which are food for the warblers and swallows!

A Diverse Island

Japan's **biodiversity** is a result of many factors. It has connected and separated from the Eurasian continent by tectonic activity many times in its existence. This has allowed plant and animal species to move onto the islands. Japan's diverse landscape provides a wide range of habitats for species to live. Isolated regions of the islands account for the high number of species found only on the islands. Many of Japan's plants and animals are endemic.

The Kujukushima Islands are a protected national park in Japan, providing space for native species to thrive.

Eco Up Close

Japanese macaques, or snow monkeys, are the only monkeys in the world to live so far north. Thick fur makes them well-adapted for a cold **climate**. Adult males weigh around 25 pounds (11 kg). They are omnivores and eat seeds, fruit, leaves, and insects. The monkeys play a large role in seed **dispersal** within the islands' ecosystems. Undigested seeds are excreted far away from the parent plant. Wild dogs and mountain hawk eagles hunt the monkeys. The macaques are also threatened by habitat loss.

Japanese macaques

Indonesian Islands

The Republic of Indonesia is located in southeast Asia in the Indian and Pacific Oceans. It is made up of 17,508 islands. Many of the islands contain unique species not found anywhere else in the world. These include birds such as the Javanese peacock and Sumatran drongo.

Rare Animals

Some of the endemic species found on these islands are extremely rare. The single-horned Javan rhinoceros is found only in one park on the western tip of Java. Like other species of rhinoceroses, **poaching** (illegal killing) has driven it to near extinction. There are many unique insect species in Indonesia, including 8-inch (20 cm) long giant walkingsticks and birdwing butterflies.

Trees and Plants

The world's largest flower, *Rafflesia arnoldii*, is also found in Indonesia. Its flowers can be up to 3 feet (0.9 m) wide. There are also hundreds of species of fig trees in Indonesia. Each fig tree has a different species of wasp responsible for its **pollination**. The two have a **mutualistic relationship**. If a particular fig tree disappears, so does the wasp. Likewise, if the wasp species disappears, its fig tree is soon lost.

There are close to 40,000 flowering plant species on the islands of Indonesia, including 5,000 species of orchids.

Eco Up Close

The Komodo dragon is a lizard that grows up to 10 feet (3 m) long. It is the largest lizard in the world. Living only on two small Indonesian islands, the Komodo dragon was not discovered until 1912. Komodo dragons are carnivores. Their favorite food is the Timor deer, but they will eat any kind of meat. Young Komodo dragons eat small lizards and insects. Komodo dragons are **apex predators**. An apex predator is an animal at the top of the food chain that has few, if any, predators of its own.

Komodo dragon

Madagascar

Madagascar is located off the southeast coast of Africa. It is one of the largest islands in the world, and is the oldest island in existence. Almost the size of Texas, its landscape includes rain forests, tropical dry forests, plateaus, and deserts. Most of the plant and animal life on the island can only be found there. Due to its isolation from the rest of the world, life evolved differently on the island.

Plant Riches

There are more than 12,000 species of unique plants in Madagascar, including eight species of the strange-looking baobab tree. These plants are producers, and many provide food for plant-eating insects and mammals. These plants also provide a habitat for the approximately 280 species of birds, 300 amphibian species, and 300 reptile species found on the island.

Forests Under Threat

Most of Madagascar's biodiversity is found in the lower forests. These same forests are cleared for crops and timber (trees grown for their wood). Only a small area of the land in Madagascar is still forested. Habitat loss, hunting, and the collection of species for illegal pet trade are affecting native animal **populations**. Conservation organizations began working hard to record new species before it was too late. From 1999 to 2010, scientists discovered 615 new species in Madagascar, including 385 plants, 41 mammals, 69 amphibians, and 61 reptiles.

More than half of Madagascar's wetlands have been lost to habitat destruction.

Eco Focus

Many of Madagascar's animals have not evolved to deal with invasive species. The biggest direct threat to the island's native wildlife is a toad. The Asian toad is an invasive species. Native animals that try to eat this poisonous toad usually die. What can be done to help reduce the introduction of invasive species? Explain your thinking.

Eco Up Close

Lemurs are insect-eating mammals. They can be found in almost all of Madagascar's ecosystems. There are 33 different species of lemurs on the island, and all of these are endemic. As a result of Madagascar's isolation, lemurs were able to evolve with little competition and few predators hunting them. All lemur species are now endangered. This is because their habitat has been destroyed.

lemur

Greenland

Greenland is the world's largest island. It covers 836,330 square miles (2,166,086 sq km). Greenland formed as Earth's shifting continents broke apart. It is mostly covered by an icecap that is several thousand feet thick.

Tough Living

The Arctic environment and ever-present ice mean that plant and animal life on Greenland is limited. As a result, land-based food chains are simple and short. Herbivores found there include the musk ox, caribou, Arctic hare, Arctic lemming, geese, grouse, and some duck species. The caribou's diet in the summer consists mainly of grasses and sedges, which are similar to grass, and **lichens** in the winter. Musk ox eat willows, sedges, and grasses.

Lemmings and the Food Chain

The Arctic lemming is a short, thick-tailed rodent that feeds on willows and grasses. The lemming is an important species in this ecosystem. It is prey for a number of predators, including the ermine, Arctic fox, and birds such as the snowy owl, jaeger, raven, and sometimes the peregrine falcon and gyrfalcon. The Arctic wolf feeds on lemmings, Arctic hares, foxes, seals on the ice, and musk ox. Some insects and other decomposers feed mainly on dead **organic** material. These nutrients are then used for the following short growing season.

Eco Focus

The Greenland ice sheet covers 660,000 square miles (1.7 million sq km) and is thousands of feet deep. Research shows the ice sheet is thinning around its edges as a result of climate change. Summer melt has increased during the past 20 years. Sea ice is also being affected. How will this affect species such as the polar bear? How will it affect oceans and coastlines? Explain your thinking.

Greenland's warming climate will change the ecosystems found there.

polar bear

Eco Up Close

Polar bears are adapted for the sea-ice habitat. They are good swimmers and can travel long distances by water when necessary. Polar bears are omnivores. When on land, they will occasionally eat vegetation, catch geese and caribou, and eat bird eggs. However, their preferred meals are harbor seals and bearded seals. When there are plenty of seals to eat, the bears eat only the seal's fat, leaving the rest of the seal for other animals. They are on top of the food chain in the Arctic environment.

Water, Water, Everywhere

Islands provide a diverse ecosystem with new species still being discovered. However, some islands are in trouble. Climate change is causing a rise in sea levels. Increasing salt content in water systems can change the ecosystem. Many people believe that gases such as carbon dioxide are causing increased temperatures and changing weather patterns. Carbon dioxide **emissions** result from human activities such as driving, heating our homes, and using electricity.

What Can You Do?

Write to your politicians. Demand action on climate change.

Start a lunchbox challenge at your school to encourage other children to eat food that is made nearby.

Reduce, reuse, and recycle to help reduce carbon dioxide emissions.

To save electricity, unplug electronic devices when they are not in use.

Take shorter showers to use less energy to heat water.

Save energy by eating local foods that do not have to be shipped long distances.

Plant a tree and take a step toward reducing carbon dioxide in the atmosphere.

Activity:

Suck It Up!

Oceans are the perfect ecosystem for many species, but what happens when salt water invades islands? Let's find out!

You Will Need:

- Three 2-quart (2-liter) plastic soda bottles, labels removed, and cut into two sections about one quarter from the top, with a small hole drilled in each lid
- Length of wicking string
- Bean seeds
- Potting soil
- Water
- Table salt
- Teaspoon
- Ruler
- Pen
- Labels

Instructions

1. Soak the wicking string in water. Thread it through the hole in the bottle top.
2. Fill the bottom (reservoir) of the bottle $1/3$ full of water.
3. Turn the bottle top upside down and put it into the bottom reservoir.

WATER

3 PERCENT SALT WATER

SALT WATER

4. Add potting soil to the top container and plant the seeds. Water the soil regularly from the top until seeds sprout.
5. Repeat steps 1 to 4 for the other two containers.
6. After seeds have sprouted, label one container "water," one "3 percent salt water," and the last one "salt water."
7. Fill the reservoir of the bottle labeled "water" with plain water.
8. Make a 3 percent saltwater solution by adding $1/4$ teaspoon of salt to 34 ounces (1 liter) of water. Use this to fill the second reservoir.
9. Make a 100 percent saltwater solution by adding 8 tsp of salt to 34 ounces (1 liter) of water. Use this to fill the third reservoir.
10. Add the appropriate liquid to each reservoir when necessary.

The Challenge

Observe the plants over the next few weeks.

- Which plants grew the best? Which ones died off?
- What does this tell you about the possible effects of rising sea levels?
- How might these results affect the rest of the food chain on an island?

Share your results with others.

Glossary

Please note: Some bold-faced words are defined in the text

abiotic factors Nonliving parts of an ecosystem, such as water and soil

adapted Changed over long periods of time or many generations, to better survive an environment

alien Foreign or not native

amphibian An animal such as a frog or salamander that begins life in water, then lives on land as an adult

bacteria Living organisms made up of only one cell

biodiversity The variety of plant and animal life in an ecosystem or other area on Earth

biotic factors Living parts of an ecosystem, such as plants and animals

calcium carbonate A chemical substance found in rocks and the shells of some sea creatures and snails

climate The normal weather in a specific area

climate change A process in which the environment changes to become warmer, colder, drier, or wetter than normal. This can occur naturally, or it can be caused by human activity

commercial fishing Fishing to make money

condensation The process in which water vapor cools and changes to liquid form

continent A landmass, or large area of land, such as North America, Asia, or Australia

coral reef A reef made from tiny sea animals that build skeletons of calcium carbonate outside their bodies

currents Strong movements of water in a certain direction

dispersal Spreading or scattering

diverse Having many different types of something

elevation Height of a location

emissions Something sent out, such as harmful gases

endemic A plant or animal found only in one country or area

estuaries Tidal mouths of large rivers and the transition zone from fresh water to salt water

evaporation The process in which water is heated by the sun and changed from a liquid into a gas called water vapor

evolved Changed over thousands of years to adapt to the surrounding conditions

excreted Passed waste out of the body

food chain A chain of organisms in which each member uses the member below as food

food web The interlinked food chains in an ecosystem

fungi Organisms, such as mold, that absorb food from their environment

gigantism Unusual or abnormal largeness

habitat The natural environment of an animal or plant

interrelationships The relationships between many different organisms and their environment

invasive species A species that is introduced into an ecosystem where it did not originally live

isolation Being apart from something

lagoons Stretches of salt water separated from the seas by a low sandbank or coral reef

lichens Types of organisms made up of fungi and algae living together in a mutualistic relationship

mainland A large area of land that may have small islands nearby

mutualistic relationship A close relationship between two or more species that benefits or helps both species

native Originating from a specific location

nutrients Substances that allow organisms to thrive and grow

organic Of, related to, or derived from living matter

organisms Living things

overgrazing Eating more grass than the ecosystem can replace

pesticide A chemical used to kill animals or insects that damage plants or crops

photosynthesis The process in which plants use sunlight to change carbon dioxide and water into food and oxygen

pollination Transfering pollen grains to part of a plant to produce new seeds

populations The total number of species in an area

precipitation Water that falls from the clouds as rain, snow, sleet, or hail

prey An animal that is hunted by another animal for food

reproduce To produce offspring

reptile An animal, such as a lizard or a snake, that has scales and that relies on the surrounding temperature to warm or cool its body

rodents Small animals that have sharp front teeth. Mice, rats, and squirrels are rodents

species A group of animals or plants that are similar and can produce young

subalpine High slopes and the zone just below the treeline

subspecies A group of animals that shares the same characteristics and can breed with other animals of the same species, but are different from the main species

tectonic plates Sections of Earth's crust that float on top of its mantle

tropical Describing a hot and humid climate

Learning More

Find out more about Earth's precious island ecosystems.

Books

Chin, Jason. *Island: A Story of the Galápagos*. New York, NY: Roaring Brook Press, 2012.

Gillespie, Rosemary G & David A. Clague. *Encyclopedia of Islands* Encyclopedias of the Natural World. Oakland, CA: University of California Press, 2009.

Kitts, Wendy. *Sable Island: The Wandering Sandbar*. Halifax, NS: Nimbus Publishing, 2012.

Websites

Visit this website to learn about some of the careers that you could choose in ecology:
http://kids.nceas.ucsb.edu/ecology/careers.html

Learn more about Darwin's islands—the Galápagos – at:
www.worldwildlife.org/places/the-galapagos

Discover more about islands at:
www.mbgnet.net/salt/sandy/index.htm

Explore the magic of Madagascar:
www.worldwildlife.org/places/madagascar

Index